Portraits
FROM NATURE
35 *Studies for Dimensional Quilts*

JEAN WELLS

C&T PUBLISHING

Text © 2006 Jean Wells

Artwork © 2006 C&T Publishing, Inc.

Publisher: Amy Marson

Editorial Director: Gailen Runge

Acquisitions Editor: Jan Grigsby

Editor: Candie Frankel

Technical Editors: Elin Thomas, Deborah Dubois

Copyeditor/Proofreader: Wordfirm Inc.

Cover Designer: Kristy K. Zacharias

Design Director/Book Designer: Kristy K. Zacharias

Illustrator: Kirstie L. Pettersen

Production Assistants: Kerry Graham, Tini Manihusan

Photography: All project photographs by C&T Publishing, Inc., All nature
photographs by Valori Wells.

Published by C&T Publishing, Inc., P.O. Box 1456, Lafayette, CA 94549

Front cover: *Herb Garden* by Jean Wells

Back cover: *Aspen Tree*, and *Fall Fantasy* by Jean Wells

Library of Congress Cataloging-in-Publication Data

Wells, Jean.

Portraits from nature : 35 studies for dimensional quilts / Jean Wells Keenan.

  p. cm.

Includes index.

ISBN-13: 978-1-57120-355-7 (paper trade : alk. paper)

ISBN-10: 1-57120-355-9 (paper trade : alk. paper)

1. Quilting--Patterns. 2. Appliqué--Patterns. 3. Nature in art. I. Title.

TT835.W4645 2006

746.46'041--dc22

2006007788

Printed in China

10 9 8 7 6 5 4 3 2 1

acknowledgments

A book is only as good as all of its parts. Candie Frankel
is a superb editor; she understands my concept of the
book and brings it to life. Hats off to Elin Thomas for
technical editing. She doesn't miss a beat, and there is a
lot to review. Kristy Zacharias, with her fresh eye for
color and design, is able to carry out my vision for the
book design. I like my books to reflect the style of the
projects. As in sewing, it's the little details that make a
book special. Thank you to the entire editorial, design,
and production team as well as to C&T Publishing for
believing in the project.

table of contents

introduction

Portraits From Nature expresses my involvement with the patterns and colors found in nature. Since childhood, I've been in love with the outdoors. Cultivated gardens, wild forests, rocky mountain streams, and sandy beaches all continue to enchant me. The sensory delights go beyond what I can see; nature's delicate balance is expressed in gentle sounds, sweet floral perfumes, and earthy, organic decay. When I make garden portraits, my passions for gardening and quilting come together in a perfect marriage.

Most of the quilts in this collection contain studies of the little things in nature, from individual flowers and leaves to a butterfly. Each element is appliquéd and framed with contrasting binding to make it appear as an individual picture. Then several of these small portraits are grouped together against a quilted background. Two quilts, *Aspen Tree* (page 46) and *Sunflowers of Provence* (page 48), feature single portraits that are larger in scale but still attentive to details. Smaller individual studies are also perfect in shadow boxes.

Subject matter for these portrait quilts abounds. The first chapter discusses how to develop a sketchbook and build a collection of photos that you can turn to for inspiration. I love working from garden photographs. As you're planning your motifs, you'll also want to start thinking about what fabrics to use and how to put together effective combinations.

The next two chapters describe how to appliqué, embellish, and bind the portraits and how to machine quilt the background. With my construction method, the portraits appear to be standing out from the surface of the quilt. Once you become acquainted with these easy techniques, you'll be able to follow the Quilt Assembly Checklist on page 21 to make any of the projects in this book. For more ideas on how to mix and match the studies, as well as how to introduce your own designs, be sure to visit the Student Gallery (pages 29–33). I know you'll enjoy this easy way to create pictures of your own garden and the larger outdoor world.

inspiration

sketchbook

As an avid gardener and quilter, I am always looking at line, pattern, and color. I gain inspiration from nature, whether I am weeding, walking along a creek, or relaxing in a chair under a pine tree. Garden magazines, books, and catalogs are a rich source of ideas, too. Beautiful garden photography from around the world inspires me to take a closer look at the details in my own backyard.

Photos and sketches from my design notebook

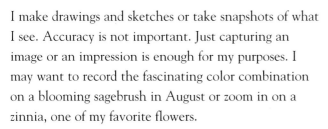

I make drawings and sketches or take snapshots of what I see. Accuracy is not important. Just capturing an image or an impression is enough for my purposes. I may want to record the fascinating color combination on a blooming sagebrush in August or zoom in on a zinnia, one of my favorite flowers.

Tracing is an easy way to start sketching on your own. Buy a pad of tracing paper and a mechanical pencil with 0.5mm lead. Start by tracing actual natural shapes that you find interesting—a leaf picked up from the forest floor or a dogwood blossom plucked from a tree on your front lawn.

When you put the tracing paper over a leaf or blossom, you won't be able to see every little detail. A blurred image is perfect, however, because it forces you to simplify the shape in preparation for fabric appliqué. For a mirror-image design, just turn over the tracing paper.

The design lines will show through the paper. Go over them in pencil to make them more visible.

Assemble your photos and sketches in a notebook or a box. Over time, you'll build a small, personal collection that you can turn to for design inspiration and reference.

portraits

I got the idea for the portraits from an etching I had seen in an art gallery. Small pictures were laid out, side by side, in a boxy format. The design was simple: small pictures contained within a larger box.

For my very first portraits project, I worked in a vertical format and used graph paper to figure out the size and sequence of shapes. It took time to get the balance right. As a quilter, I was inclined to allow an even margin of fabric all around, like the borders on a quilt. But I soon discovered that a slightly wider margin on the bottom made the entire piece look better.

Professional framers use this same trick when they cut mats for photographs and prints.

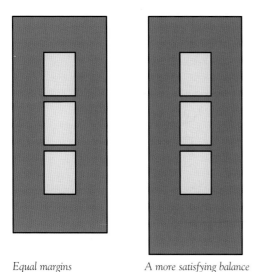

Equal margins   A more satisfying balance

To ensure that I have enough background fabric, I usually cut a larger piece than I think I will need, knowing that I can trim it to the final size later. When the portraits are complete, I arrange them on the background, study the composition, and make any adjustments. You won't have to do this for the quilt projects in this book, because the portrait dimensions are already calculated, but if you design your own projects, this is a good tip to keep in mind.

You can also maneuver images *within* the portraits. The "safe" approach is to place whole images inside a square or rectangle. For drama, let a shape spill off the edge and then crop it with the binding, much as you would use your camera's view finder to crop in for a close-up. Cropped images are dynamic because of the tension they create; the eye strains to see the part of the picture that is missing. Just a few cropped images in the entire quilt are all it takes to add this energetic spark. A photocopier that enlarges and reduces is invaluable for resizing shapes to help achieve this effect.

fabric palette

In addition to the appliqués, three key fabrics are needed for each project:

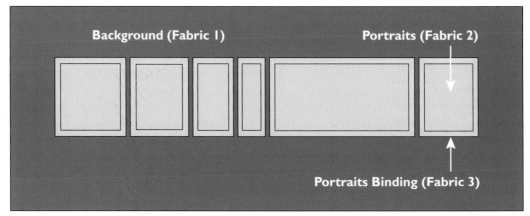

Background (Fabric 1)   Portraits (Fabric 2)

Portraits Binding (Fabric 3)

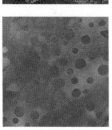

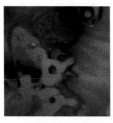

Your goal is to put together combinations that create visual excitement and make the portraits stand out. Fortunately, quilting cottons come in a variety of styles and colors. In general, look for solids or patterns that will be easy to "read" in the larger composition. Examples include low-contrast textures (semisolids), hand-painted textures, monochromatics, painterly style textures, and small prints. Once in a while, I find a large print with areas of solidlike texture that I can use. If the fabric is plain, try stitching and beads to add texture to the appliqué.

palette tips

APPLIQUÉS Choose a variety of medium colors.

PORTRAITS AND BACKGROUND Choose one light fabric and one dark fabric. Decide which fabric will be for the portraits and which will be for the background.

PORTRAITS BINDING Choose a fabric that is lighter, brighter, or darker than the portraits fabric and the background fabric. Look for interesting color or texture contrasts.

I audition fabrics until I find a combination that works. Many times, I surprise myself! On *Zinnias* (page 44), I was at a loss when it came to the portraits binding. I felt I had used up all my color options in the appliqués. Then, while wandering through my fabric stash, I came upon the plaid you see around the edges. The colors were perfect, and the bias-cut strips added rhythm to the blocks. This fabric find was a happy accident.

The portrait binding for *Aspen Tree* (page 46) really had me stumped. I kept trying to add another color to the palette, but nothing was working. Finally, I tried a deeper value of the orange leaves. I used a hand-dyed fabric that was very splotchy. When cut up, it introduced little bits of yellow here and there that picked up on the leaves in the interior.

Portraits binding fabric from Zinnias

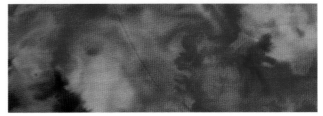

Portrait binding fabric from Aspen Tree

Butterfly Garden (page 42) was an artistic stretch for me. I had originally planned a melon color background, but when I placed the completed portraits on top of my fabric, the composition just didn't work. I have learned that if I can't come up with a solution at the moment, the best thing is to set the piece—and the problem—aside for a day or two until an idea takes shape. At times like this, your collection of pictures comes in handy. Thumb through your notebook or box. You'll usually find that a sketch or picture you have looked at perhaps dozens of times before will suddenly jump out at you and give you a new idea or direction to explore. Then go visit your fabric stash. The answer for me this time around was a sky fabric hand dyed by Mickey Lawler of Skydyes.

Make sure you choose tightly woven fabrics, especially for the smallest appliqué shapes. Loosely woven fabrics will fray along the edges and become difficult to handle. You can use fibers other than cotton, as long as you can sew a satin stitch around the edge of the appliqué. Make a test appliqué before investing time and money in an unusual fabric.

Background fabric in Butterfly Garden

Hand-dyed fabrics work like batiks to add naturalistic texture. Last summer, I took a sun-printing class and created some fun fabrics. One of my sky prints became the portraits fabric in Shirley Poppies.

creating the portraits

The "portraits" in my quilts are actually small appliquéd pictures. This chapter explains how to cut and prepare the appliqués, how to apply decorative stitching and beads, and how to frame the edges with bias binding.

What You'll Need

PAPER-BACKED FUSIBLE WEB

Fusible web allows you to use your iron to fuse appliqué shapes to one another or to the portrait fabric. I prefer fusible products that appear as dots or a web rather than a continuous film, which can be difficult to stitch through. Purchase a lightweight fusible web so the appliqués do not become bulky. The paper backing must be plain, without any waxy coating. I use 40″-wide fusible web. If you choose a web product that has a different width, you may need to adjust the yardage requirements in the project materials lists.

APPLIQUÉ PRESSING SHEET

An appliqué pressing sheet is a flexible silicone or Teflon sheet that can withstand high heat. Use it at the ironing board when assembling and fusing appliqués. Sandwich the appliqué between two pressing sheets or between the layers of a folded pressing sheet to prevent any oozing fusible from damaging the surface of the ironing board or the soleplate of the iron.

WASHABLE GLUE STICK

Use a washable glue stick to temporarily baste the appliqués and binding in place before sewing.

LIGHTWEIGHT TEARAWAY STABILIZER

Lightweight tearaway stabilizer resembles interfacing. It is sold by the yard or in packages of precut sheets. Layer the stabilizer under the portrait fabric to strengthen and stabilize the fabric during machine appliqué. After you have finished sewing the appliqué, tear off the excess stabilizer and discard.

making the appliques

Select the appliqué designs for your nature portraits from the patterns (pages 52–69). Follow the projects instructions or combine the designs any way you wish. Keep in mind that the appliqué shapes will be reversed when fused in place. As you gain experience, you may want to create your own designs.

Once you have selected a design, study it to determine how many different appliqué shapes are used. Choose a fabric for each shape and for the portraits background, as described in Fabric Palette (page 8). Follow the steps below to make each appliqué.

1. **Mark the fusible web.** Place the fusible web, paper side up, on the appliqué pattern. Use a pencil to trace an appliqué shape from the pattern. Reposition the fusible web on the pattern and trace another shape, spacing the traced shapes at least ½″ apart. Add roughly ¼″ to the edges of pieces that will underlap other pieces in the portrait. Continue in this way until you have made a separate tracing for each shape in the pattern. Be sure to group together shapes that will be cut from the same fabric.

2. **Rough cut the fusible web.** Cut out the fusible web shapes roughly ¼″ beyond the marked lines. You may cut out shapes for the same fabric as a group.

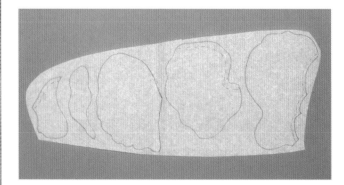

3. **Fuse the web pattern to the fabric.** Place the fabric for your first appliqué shape face down on the ironing board. Place the pattern paper side up on the fabric, so the rough side of the fusible web is against the wrong side of the fabric. Follow the manufacturer's instructions to heat the iron and fuse the pattern to the fabric. Let the appliqué cool. Do not remove the paper backing. Repeat for all the appliqué shapes, using a variety of fabrics. For easier handling, fuse grouped shapes as a unit.

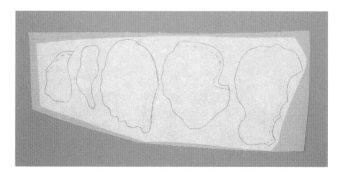

4. Cut out the appliqués. Using sharp scissors, cut out each appliqué shape on the pencil outline.

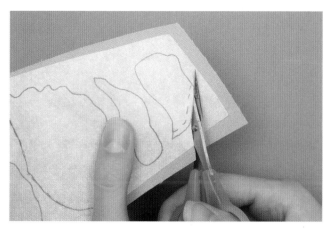

5. Peel off the paper backing. If the paper doesn't readily release, run a pin across it to loosen it.

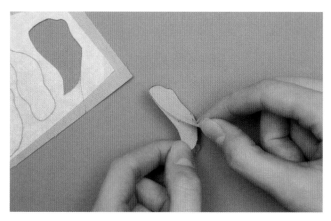

6. Compose the appliqués. Arrange the appliqué pieces on the pressing sheet. Refer to the original pattern for placement of overlapping shapes, such as petals, leaves, and butterfly wings. Once you are satisfied with the placement, layer a second pressing sheet on top (or fold the pressing sheet over onto itself), sandwiching the appliqué in between. Press to fuse the appliqués

together. Let cool. You can now pick up the appliqué as a single unit.

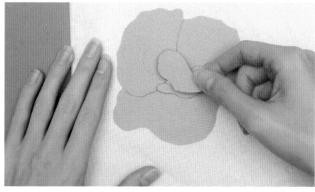

7. Assemble the portrait. Place the appliqué on the appropriate portrait block, right sides facing up. Fuse in place. Let cool.

artistic stitching

Decorative machine stitching is essential for a professionally rendered appliqué. Stitching does more than hold down the edges. It adds lines of color and texture. In addition, the tactile quality of stitching gives flowers and leaves a hint of realism. There are several stitches I like to use, but you may discover others on your sewing machine.

Satin Stitch

Satin stitch is a very closely spaced zigzag stitch. Stitching done in a darker, lighter, or bolder thread color than the adjacent fabrics will create a strong visual outline around the appliqué shape. Stitching done in a matching thread color will blend in. You can adjust the width of the satin stitch from narrow to wide—narrow for a small appliqué and wide for a large appliqué. If your sewing machine has a movable stitch-width dial, you can actually change the stitch width as you sew. I like to use this feature to sew leaf vein lines, because it lets me taper the stitching to a sharp point. I also use it to define the tips of pointed leaves and petals.

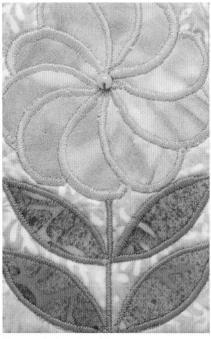

Satin-stitched petals and leaves

Start by consulting your sewing machine manual and setting the machine to a normal zigzag satin stitch. Slip tearaway stabilizer under a piece of scrap fabric and sew for a few inches to test your setting. Check the thread coverage. If the thread matches the fabric, the coverage may be fine. If you are using contrasting thread, you may need to make the stitches closer together to prevent the fabric edges from peeking through. I usually make the stitches a little bit closer than recommended, regardless of the thread color, so that the stitching truly does look like smooth satin. When you find a look you like, jot down the machine settings for future reference.

having trouble?

If your machine does not sew a smooth satin stitch, it may need a tension adjustment. The top tension can be loosened so the upper thread wraps through to the underside. If you are unable to make these adjustments on your own, take your machine and a sample of your work to a sewing machine technician and explain what you are trying to achieve. I have my machine tuned up two or three times a year, as I do lots of sewing.

To sew the appliqués, place a piece of tearaway stabilizer against the wrong side of the portrait fabric. Pin from the right side. Begin stitching on a straight or slightly curved edge. Set the needle to the far right zigzag position and align it with the edge of the appliqué. Lower the presser foot and begin sewing. Guide the fabric by looking in front of the presser foot. If you look where the needle goes in and out, by the time the fabric reaches the needle, it's too late to make a correction!

At an outside corner, stitch all the way to the end of the appliqué, right up to the new edge. Stop with the needle in the down position at the outside edge of the appliqué. Lift the presser foot and pivot the fabric. Lower the foot and resume stitching on the new edge.

Treat tips of leaves as outside corners.

On an inside corner, stitch to the point and stop with the needle in the fabric. Pivot and continue stitching. This technique creates a V shape on the appliqué.

Inside corners on a leaf

To sew overlapping appliqués, begin with the shapes at the back and work forward, following the same order as for fusing. Each new line of stitching will cover the ends of the preceding line, leaving a clean edge.

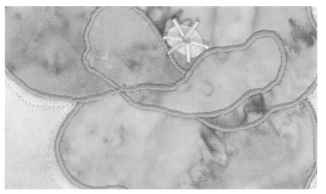

Overlapping shapes

After you finish appliquéing, pull all loose threads to the back of the fabric, tie them off, and clip the ends. Use a seam ripper to help tear away the excess stabilizer.

Decorative Stitches

Many sewing machines have decorative stitch settings that work well in machine appliqué. These stitches can be added alongside or on top of satin stitch. My favorites are blanket stitch and a scalloping design. Machine blanket stitch simulates a hand-worked blanket stitch. The stitching proceeds along the edge of the appliqué and dips in every third or fourth stitch. The scalloping stitch creates tiny crescent shapes that join at the ends.

Blanket stitch imitates the hairs on the stem of a poppy plant.

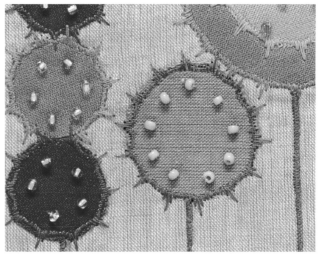

Scalloping stitch suggests organic plant growth, especially when sewn in a circle.

Detail Stitching

After you sew the appliqués to the portrait fabric, you may wish to enhance the design with more stitching. For dimension, apply a piece of thin fusible batting to the back of the portrait fabric. Then stitch from the right side, either within the appliqué or outside on the portrait fabric. Echo quilting in the portrait fabric will enhance and enliven the appliqué shape.

Echo quilting accentuates the appliqué shapes.

Use a regular presser foot to sew straight lines and a free-motion foot or embroidery foot to sew curved or irregular lines. I don't drop the feed dogs when I use a free-motion foot—I find I have more control leaving them up.

If you feel unsure about your ability to "draw" simple shapes with the sewing machine needle, place a sheet of tracing paper over the appliqué and draw some design lines onto it for practice. You may not realize it, but tracing in this way helps you memorize the lines and shape.

This simple exercise has given me the confidence to try drawing directly with the machine needle. You can also lightly mark with a pencil directly on the fabric.

Trace before you sew to memorize the stitching path.

Tendrils and leaf veining are machine stitched with contrasting thread colors.

bead embellishment

Beadwork is done by hand with needle and thread. You can use beads to depict pistils and stamens or similar details. Beads bring sparkle and luster to the portrait and enhance the stitching.

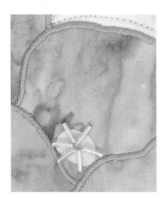

Yellow bugle beads add dimensional pistils to an appliquéd poppy.

A beading needle is long, thin, and somewhat flexible. Make sure the needle shaft is slender enough to pass through the bead hole. Pull the needle up from the fabric, slip on a bead, insert the needle back into the fabric, and pull it through to the wrong side. Knot the thread on the underside before proceeding to the next bead. Knotting after each stitch prevents all the beads from working loose should one become detached.

the portrait frame

Each portrait is framed with a 1¼″-wide binding strip. The strip is sewn to the right side of the portrait and folded over the raw edge onto the back. Because the back is stitched to the quilt, there's no need to finish the edge of the binding that is concealed. I use an easy-to-sew method to miter the corners of the binding.

1. Trim the portrait block to the exact dimensions listed in the project instructions. Remember that close cropping enhances the finished portrait.

2. Trim one end of the binding strip at a 45° angle. Fold in the cut end about ⅜″ to the wrong side.

3. Place the binding strip on the lower edge of the portrait, with right sides together and raw edges matching. Stitch exactly ¼″ from the edge until the needle is exactly ¼″ from the corner, then backtack. Lift the presser foot and needle, and clip the threads.

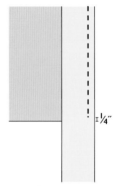

Backtack ¼″ from the corner.

4. Rotate the portrait a quarter turn on the machine bed. Fold the binding at a right angle to the edge just sewn, then bring it down even with the new edge.

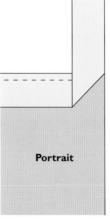 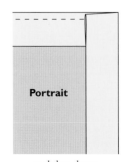

Fold the binding up . . .   . . . and then down.

5. Stitch from the top edge to exactly ¼″ from the next corner. Backtack and clip the threads as in Step 3.

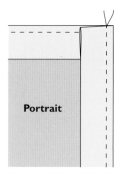

Start stitching at the edge.

6. Repeat steps 4 and 5, continuing to sew a precise ¼″ seam allowance around the edge of the portrait. At the starting point, overlap the ends of the binding by ⅜″ and stitch through all layers. Clip the threads. Trim the excess binding at a 45° angle.

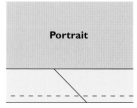

Make a neat finish.

7. Fold the binding onto the back of the portrait, creating a neat ¼″-wide frame around the image on the right side. Each corner will make a neat self-miter. Press to crease the edge. Use a washable glue stick to secure the binding on the back.

Each corner will self-miter.

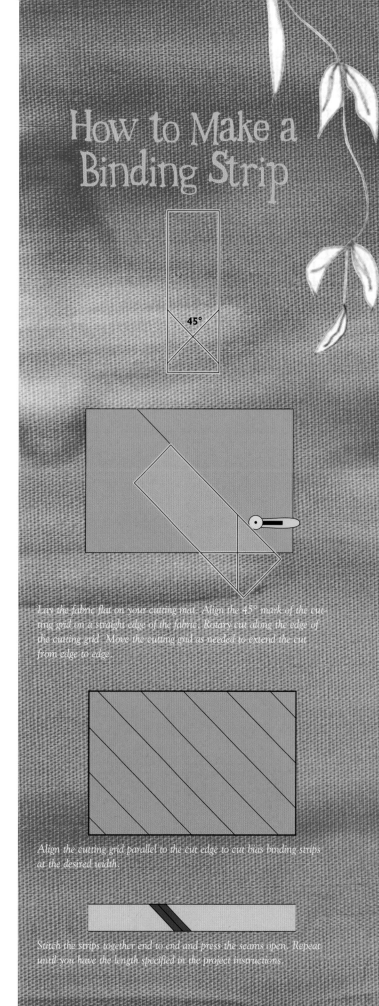

How to Make a Binding Strip

Lay the fabric flat on your cutting mat. Align the 45° mark of the cutting grid on a straight edge of the fabric. Rotary cut along the edge of the cutting grid. Move the cutting grid as needed to extend the cut from edge to edge.

Align the cutting grid parallel to the cut edge to cut bias binding strips at the desired width.

Stitch the strips together end to end and press the seams open. Repeat until you have the length specified in the project instructions.

Quilting in Motion

The portrait quilt is not complete until you have assembled the background and attached the portraits to it. The background is an important part of the overall composition. Quilters instinctively add border strips to their quilts to frame the design. In a portrait quilt, a similar concept is at play.

The background functions a bit like a picture mat with multiple openings, but the construction is much easier. The portraits are mounted on *top* of the background; there is no additional cutting or piecing.

how to layer a quilt

Lay the backing fabric wrong side up on a flat surface. Place the batting on top and pat it down without stretching it. Place the background fabric right side up on the batting. Pin through all three layers with straight pins or safety pins every 4″ or so. Layer smaller quilt sandwiches to use for practice sewing in the same way.

background quilting

The Inspiration chapter (page 6) discusses how to choose a background fabric that shows off the portrait blocks. A subtler aspect of the background is the quilting. I like to use free-motion quilting in the background. Once I start sewing, I develop a rhythm. Free-motion stitching is fast and easy to do, and it makes the overall quilt more interesting. If you tried echo quilting on the portraits blocks, you're off to a good start.

Choose a design theme that relates to the portraits. In garden-themed quilts, leafy shapes, floral motifs, and vines are almost always good choices. Continuous-line designs or motifs that you can connect without breaking the line of stitching work best. If you are nervous about

sewing without a pattern, trace the quilting designs from the patterns or scout out your own floral shapes and leaves from garden magazines or catalogs to copy.

Tracing is an important exercise. It helps you become familiar with the contours. When you draw design lines on tracing paper, you are rehearsing how you will stitch these lines and shapes later on. Some quilters like to lightly sketch a design onto fabric with chalk or a fine pencil, but I prefer—and encourage—a more spontaneous approach.

For free-motion quilting, you can use matching or contrasting thread, depending on the level of contrast desired. Use a free-motion foot or embroidery foot, just as you did for echo quilting. The feed dogs can be up or down—whichever works better for you. Sewing on a practice piece is useful, no matter how experienced you are. Get into the habit of layering your leftover fabric and batting into a mini quilt sandwich. Use your practice piece to try out your design ideas and to develop your free-motion sewing skills. Whenever I sit down to sew, I like to warm up on my practice piece before sewing the actual quilt.

Once you begin sewing on the background fabric, keep going until the entire surface is quilted. Try to relax and ease into the rhythm of your design. The goal is not to stitch every motif exactly the same but to create a harmonious whole. Keep in mind where the portraits will be placed and where the frame or binding will fall; you don't want your best quilting work to be hidden or cut off!

Free-motion quilting

to bind or to frame?

There are two ways to finish the outer edge of a portrait quilt: binding and professional framing. Binding is done after the background is quilted but before the portrait blocks are attached. Framing is done after the entire quilt is finished. Both options are included in the project instructions.

For a bound edge, trim the quilt to the dimensions given in the project instructions. Fold the quilt binding strip in half, right side out, and press. Sew the binding around the edge of the quilt, raw edges together, using a ¼″ seam allowance. Overlap the ends for a neat finish, as you did for the individual portraits. Fold the binding onto the back of the quilt and press, allowing the corners to self-miter. With matching thread, hand sew the folded edge of the binding to the back of the quilt.

Professional framing is more expensive than binding, but it gives a quilt a formal art gallery look. After you quilt the background, lightly mark the outline of the finished quilt on it. Do not trim the quilt in any way; the extra fabric allowance is needed for proper mounting in the frame. Attach the portrait blocks as directed, then take the finished quilt and the quilt diagram to a professional framer. The diagram will help you and the framer confirm the size of the frame and the placement of the quilt within it. The framer may need anywhere from a few days to several weeks to complete the job.

picture perfect

Arranging and attaching the portrait blocks is your final sewing step. Lay the quilted background on a flat surface. Referring to the quilt diagram, measure from the bound edge or the frame chalk line to place the portraits. Allow ¼″ to ½″ between each portrait block. Note that the background margin at the bottom is slightly wider than the margins at the top and sides.

Use a washable glue stick to "baste" the portraits in place. A few dabs of glue on the reverse side of the portrait should be sufficient; use more glue for larger blocks. Avoid pinning through multiple layers of batting, as this tends to skew the blocks. Use monofilament to stitch each portrait in-the-ditch along the binding seam. Use clear monofilament for light to medium colors and smoky monofilament for dark colors.

Stitch in-the-ditch.

Quilt Assembly Checklist

Here is a quick step-by-step guide for making a portraits quilt. Gather the materials listed in the project instructions, cut the fabrics as directed, and prepare the binding strips. Then follow the steps below to assemble the quilt. Specific sizes and colors are given with each project. If you need help, refer to the technique section referenced at the end of each step. You can also use this checklist when designing your own portrait quilts.

1. Prepare the appliqués. Refer to the patterns (pages 52–69). Choose one or more designs for each portrait block. Cut and fuse the selected appliqué pieces to each portrait block. (*Making the Appliqués*, page 12)

2. Sew the appliqués. Machine sew around the edges of the appliqué shapes in satin stitch or blanket stitch. Stitch in details, such as leaf veins. (*Artistic Stitching*, page 13)

3. Add beaded embellishment. Embellish the flower centers, edges of petals, and other areas as desired with beads. See the patterns and photographs for design ideas. (*Bead Embellishment*, page 16)

4. Trim the portrait blocks. Use a rotary cutter and cutting grid. Cut to the sizes listed in the project instructions. Accuracy is very important for the finished portraits to look good when grouped together in the quilt. (*The Portrait Frame*, page 16)

5. Bind the portrait blocks. Bind each portrait block using the Fabric 3 binding strip. (*The Portrait Frame*, page 16)

6. Quilt the background. Layer the quilt backing, batting, and background. Work free-motion quilting over the background. (*How to Layer a Quilt* and *Background Quilting*, page 19)

7. Bind the edge. Trim the quilt to size and bind with the Fabric 1 binding strip. For a framed quilt, lightly mark the finished size but do not trim. If you are having the quilt professionally framed, first complete Step 8. (*To Bind or to Frame?*, page 20)

8. Attach the portrait blocks. Arrange the portrait blocks as shown in the quilt diagram. Stitch in-the-ditch with monofilament. (*Picture Perfect*, page 20)

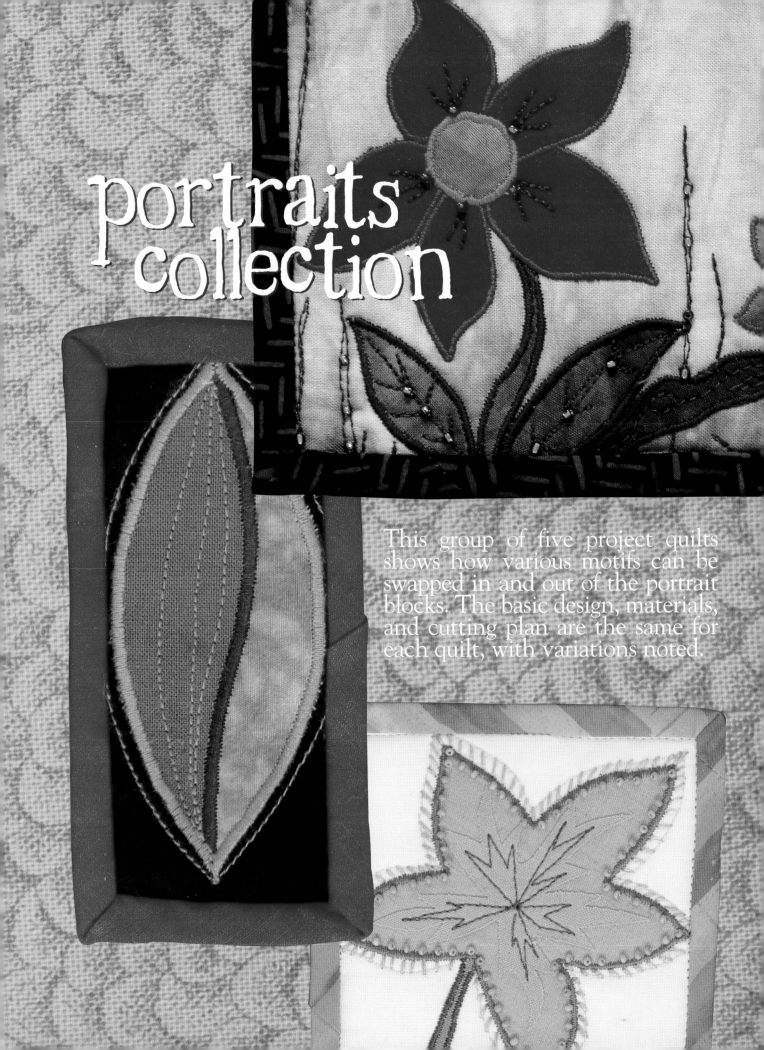

portraits
collection

This group of five project quilts shows how various motifs can be swapped in and out of the portrait blocks. The basic design, materials, and cutting plan are the same for each quilt, with variations noted.

quilt diagram

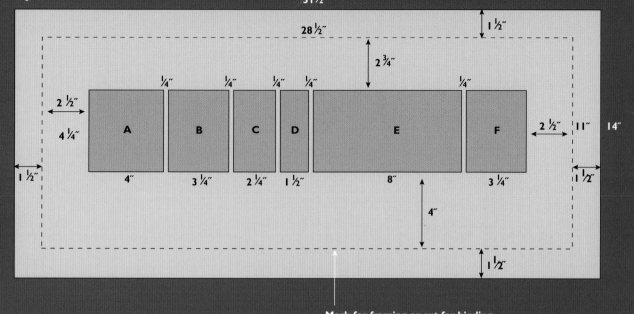

Mark for framing or cut for binding

materials

- 1¼ yards for background, backing, and quilt binding (Fabric 1)

- ¼ yard for portrait blocks (Fabric 2)

- ⅓ yard for portraits binding (Fabric 3)

- ⅓ yard for contrasting quilt binding (optional)

- Assorted ⅛-yard cuts or scraps for appliqués

- Assorted rocailles and bugle beads for embellishment

- Thread to match or slightly contrast with appliqués

- Monofilament

- ½ yard lightweight paper-backed fusible web

- ¼ yard tearaway stabilizer

- 31½″ × 14″ thin quilt batting

- Lightweight fusible batting for back of portraits (optional)

cutting guide

Fabric 1

BACKGROUND 31½″ × 14″

BACKING 31½″ × 14″

QUILT BINDING 2¼″ × 90″ long; omit if quilt will be professionally framed (*How to Make a Binding Strip*, page 17)

Fabric 2

PORTRAIT BLOCKS

A 5″ × 5″   C 3″ × 5″   E 9″ × 5″
B 4″ × 5″   D 2½″ × 5″   F 4″ × 5″

Fabric 3

PORTRAITS BINDING 1¼″ × 144″ long
(*How to Make a Binding Strip*, page 17)

assembly

Follow steps 1–8 of the checklist on page 21.

In Step 4, trim the blocks to these sizes:

A 4″ × 4¼″   C 2¼″ × 4¼″   E 8″ × 4¼″
B 3¼″ × 4¼″   D 1½″ × 4¼″   F 3¼″ × 4¼″

In Step 7, trim or mark the quilt to finish at 28½″ × 11″.

portraits from the garden

Portraits From the Garden, 28½″ × 11″, 2005, Jean Wells

An array of flowers from my garden moved to my sketchbook and finally to these appliquéd block studies.

Machine quilting on the background adds lots of leafy green foliage. This quilt uses a dark green mottled print for Fabric 1, a light green print for Fabric 2, and a coral print for Fabric 3.

THE PORTRAIT BLOCK DESIGNS ARE:

A Starflower (page 53)

B Droopy Sunflower 1 (page 53);
   cut size 5″ × 5″; trim finished block
   to 3¾″ × 4¼″

C Leaf (page 53)

D Bud (page 53)

E Gloxinia (page 53) and Trio
   (page 54)

F Chrysanthemum (page 54); trim
   finished block to 2¾″ × 4¼″

leaves

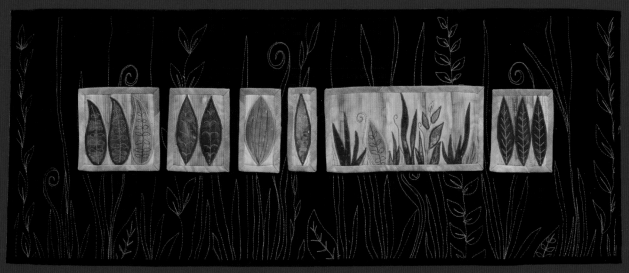

Leaves, 30½″ × 12″, 2005, Jean Wells

I am always looking for interesting stitching lines to suggest leaf veining.

These leaves, in assorted green fabrics, look especially fresh and vibrant against the orange batik chosen for Fabric 2. More light green appears in the Fabric 3 portraits binding. Fabric 1 is a black solid that shows off both the portraits and the exuberant free-motion background quilting. Note that the overall dimensions of this quilt are slightly larger than listed in the general instructions. Cut the background and the backing 34″ × 15″ to start, then finish at 30½″ × 12″.

THE PORTRAIT BLOCK DESIGNS ARE:

A Leaf Trio (page 55)

B Leaf Duo (page 54)

C Wide Leaf (page 54)

D Slender Leaf (page 54)

E Leafy Garden (page 55)

F Slender Leaf Trio (page 55)

fall fantasy

Fall Fantasy, 28½″ × 11″, 2005, Jean Wells

Fall Fantasy was made for a friend who loves red and vintage colors. I wanted to use her favorite colors in a quilt that could be framed for her new home.

I like how the free-motion quilting, done in black thread, shows up against the camel background. This quilt uses a camel solid for Fabric 1, a black solid for Fabric 2, a red solid for Fabric 3, and assorted reds, yellows, purples, and greens for the appliqués.

THE PORTRAIT BLOCK DESIGNS ARE:

A Zinnia (page 56)

B Droopy Sunflower 2 (page 56)

C Leaf (page 53)

D Bud (page 53)

E Lazy Daisy 1 (page 56), Bud Trio (page 56), and Posey (page 57)

F Cornflower (page 57)

vintage french

Vintage French, *28¹/₂″ × 11″, 2005, Jean Wells*

When my friend Betsy announced her engagement, I started thinking about what I could give her and Norm for a wedding gift.

One day, when I was visiting her quilting studio, a swatch of fabric caught my eye. Betsy had used this fabric to recover a chair for her living room. I "borrowed" it when she wasn't looking to develop my color palette for *Vintage French*: dark green mottled for Fabric 1, a white solid for Fabric 2, a pink stripe for Fabric 3, and assorted pinks, yellows, reds, and greens for the appliqués.

THE PORTRAIT BLOCK DESIGNS ARE:

A Amaryllis 1 (page 57)

B Strawberry (page 57)

C Wildflowers (page 58)

D Slender Leaf (page 54)

E Amaryllis 2 (page 58); add leaves to fill space

F Amaryllis 3 (page 59)

woodland garden

Woodland Garden, 28½″ × 11″, 2005, Jean Wells

Fall is a beautiful time in the woods, and I often take my camera with me when I go for walks.

Rich red tones—some deep, some orangy—are dominant in snapshots I have taken over the years. I looked for fabrics to capture these vibrant shades. I then set them against a green ground. The background is a woven homespun stripe quilted to resemble wood grain.

THE PORTRAIT BLOCK DESIGNS ARE:

A Zinnia (page 56)

B Lazy Daisy 2 (page 59)

C Slender Leaf (page 54)

D Wild Berries (page 58)

E Woodland Flowers (page 58)

F Wide Leaf (page 54)

student gallery

When I present my garden portrait quilts to a quilting class, I can practically see the wheels turning in my students' minds. My students bring their own perspective and interests to the work they do, and the results go far beyond gardening. They have convinced me to continue exploring new subjects for these small appliquéd portraits.

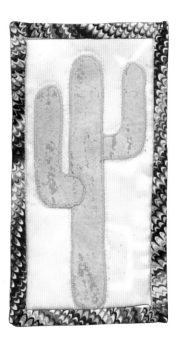
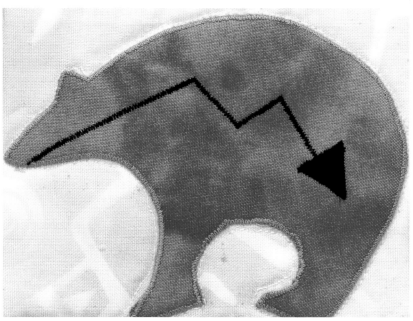

Southwest, $28^{1}/_{2}″ \times 18″$, 2005, Nikki Cooper. Nikki attended the first Portraits From the Garden class I ever taught. For her first project, a Hawaiian-themed quilt, she fused flowers cut from a printed fabric. For her second quilt, she designed desert and American Indian motifs in a Southwestern theme. The portraits vary in height and width, and the entire arrangement is anchored at the base by a long band of chili peppers.

French Connection, 30½″ × 12″, 2005, Jeanne Sellgren.
Jeanne's country French kitchen is the perfect setting for this bright quilt. Jeanne added a rooster and a topiary to the flower patterns introduced in class. The diagonal plaid background adds a homey touch and gave Jeanne easy-to-follow stitching lines for the machine quilting.

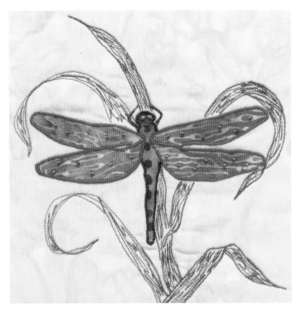

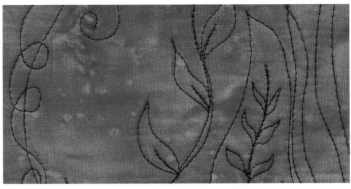

Along the Riverbank, 26½″ × 14″, 2005, Ann Richardson. An avid outdoorswoman who loves river rafting, Ann enjoys seeing butterflies and dragonflies at the water's edge. Her appliqué motifs repeat in the exquisite free-motion quilting, done in brown thread on a turquoise background. Ann was originally going for a vertical orientation, but the quilting designs worked better when the piece was laid out horizontally. Note that the portrait bindings are worked in several colors, rather than just one.

Halloween sewing-machine cover, *24″ × 14″, 2005, Joyce Boyd, sewn from a Cotton Ginny's pattern. Joyce loves pumpkins and can be counted on to give her quilting projects a fall theme. She transformed one of my flower designs into a sun by adding radiating quilting lines. A light green striped fabric makes a perfect leaf, especially when the stripes are placed on the diagonal. More pumpkins and leaves are free-motion quilted.*

shirley poppies

I love visiting garden centers in the spring when the Shirley poppies are in bloom. To make my appliquéd poppies as realistic as possible, I choose the same vibrant colors seen in nature and then sew bugle beads to the surface for the pistils. The fabric stems are edged first in satin stitch and then in blanket stitch to suggest surface fuzz. Last spring, I made a point of sketching the leaves on my poppy plants to get ideas for free-motion quilting. I tried to create the illusion that the poppy plants are actually growing out of this quilted background. *Shirley Poppies* is constructed like the quilts in the Portraits Collection (pages 22–28), except that all the portraits feature the same image and are the same size.

materials

I ¼ yards for background and backing; add ⅓ yard for optional quilt binding (Fabric I)

¼ yard for portrait blocks (Fabric 2)

⅓ yard for portraits binding (Fabric 3)

5 assorted ⅛-yard cuts including yellow, for poppies and poppy centers

⅛ yard or scrap for stems

Light yellow bugle beads for embellishment

Thread to match or slightly contrast with appliqués

Monofilament

Thread slightly darker than background for quilting

½ yard lightweight paper-backed fusible web

½ yard tearaway stabilizer

40″ × 20″ thin quilt batting or lightweight fusible batting, plus extra for portrait blocks

cutting guide

Fabric 1

BACKGROUND 40″ × 20″

BACKING 40″ × 20″

QUILT BINDING 2¼″ × 118″ long; omit if quilt will be professionally framed (*How to Make a Binding Strip*, page 17)

Fabric 2

Cut 5 pieces, each 6½″ × 7½″, for portrait blocks A, B, C, D, and E.

Fabric 3

PORTRAITS BINDING 1¼″ × 150″ long (*How to Make a Binding Strip*, page 17)

assembly

Follow steps 1–8 of the checklist on page 21.

Use the Poppy pattern (page 59). Make the poppy for each portrait a different color. Appliqué a yellow fabric oval at the center of each poppy and embellish with yellow bugle beads.

In Step 4, trim each portrait block to 5″ × 6″.

In Step 7, trim or mark the quilt for 37″ × 17″.

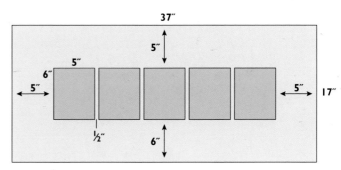

Quilt Diagram

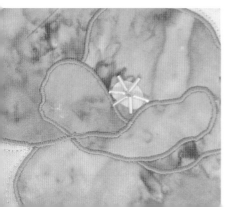
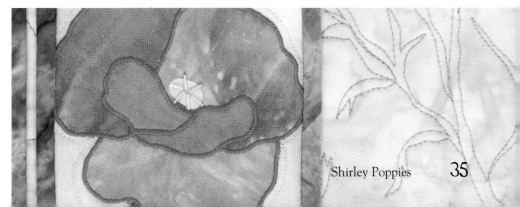

olivia's garden

The flowers in this retro-style "lollipop" garden quilt are circles—lots of them!—in different sizes and colors. The portrait blocks are different colors, too. I chose the palette to match the nursery furnishings of my new granddaughter, Olivia Rose. Straight quilting lines with occasional circles repeat the appliqué shapes in the background.

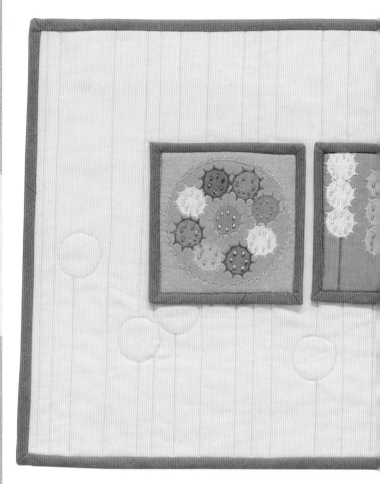

materials

1 yard for background and backing (Fabric 1)

Assorted ¼-yard cuts or scraps for portrait blocks and appliqués (Fabric 2 group)

½ yard for quilt and portraits binding (Fabric 3)

Assorted beads to match appliqué fabrics

Thread to match or slightly contrast with appliqués

Monofilament

½ yard lightweight paper-backed fusible web

¼ yard tearaway stabilizer

½ yard thin quilt batting or lightweight fusible batting

cutting guide

Fabric 1

BACKGROUND 38½″ × 16″

BACKING 38½″ × 16″

Fabric 2 Group

PORTRAIT BLOCKS:

A 5½″ × 5½″   D 2½″ × 5½″

B 4½″ × 5½″   E 9½″ × 5½″

C 3½″ × 5½″   F 4½″ × 5½″

Fabric 3

PORTRAITS BINDING 1¼″ × 140″ long (*How to Make a Binding Strip*, page 17)

QUILT BINDING 2¼″ × 105″ long; omit if quilt will be professionally framed (*How to Make a Binding Strip*, page 17)

Olivia's Garden, 35¹/₂″ × 13″, 2005, Jean Wells

assembly

Follow steps 1–8 of the checklist on page 21.

Use the Circle Flower appliqué patterns A–E on pages 66–67. Refer to the block diagrams on page 38 for appliqué placement.

In Step 4, trim the blocks to the following sizes:

A 4¹/₂″ × 4¹/₂″   D 1¹/₂″ × 4¹/₂″

B 3¹/₂″ × 4¹/₂″   E 8¹/₂″ × 4¹/₂″

C 2¹/₂″ × 4¹/₂″   F 3¹/₂″ × 4¹/₂″

In Step 7, trim or mark the quilt for 35¹/₂″ × 13″. Use the 2¹/₄″-wide binding strip cut from Fabric 3 to bind the quilt.

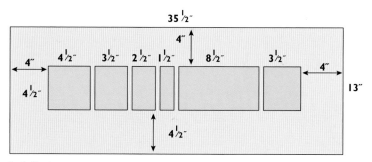

Quilt Diagram

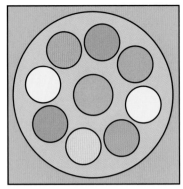

Block A

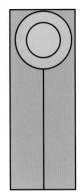

Block D

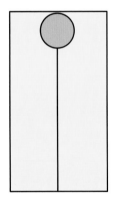

Block B

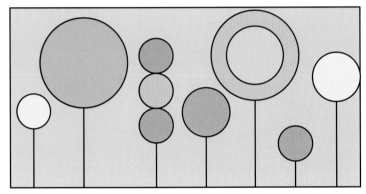

Block E

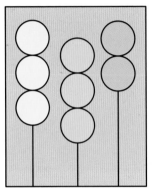

Block C

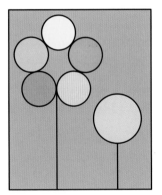

Block F

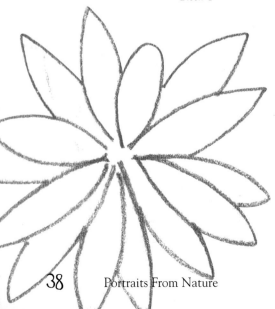

herb garden

Herbs play a big role in my garden. I find inspiration in their hearty shapes. Most herbs will last out our cold winters and become even stronger the next year. This quilt celebrates the simple plant profiles that, put together, create a lush, rustic garden. The playful, irregular shapes of the blocks add to this quilt's organic appeal.

Herb Garden, 24″ × 28″, 2005, Jean Wells

cutting guide

Fabric 1

BACKGROUND 28″ × 31½″

BACKING 28″ × 31½″

Fabric 2 Group

Use block patterns A, B, C, and D (pages 60–61). Cut an irregular block from each fabric.

Fabric 3

PORTRAITS BINDING 1¼″ × 160″ long (*How to Make a Binding Strip*, page 17)

Fabric 4

QUILT BINDING 2¼″ × 124″ long; omit if quilt will be professionally framed (*How to Make a Binding Strip*, page 17)

assembly

Follow steps 1–8 of the checklist on page 21.

Use the patterns on pages 62–65 to cut the appliqués for four portrait blocks. The portrait designs are:

A Five-Petal Flower (page 62)

B Large Nine-Petal Flower (page 65)

C Large Echinacea Pair (page 64)

D Leaf Spears (make 3) and Small Leaves (make 13) (page 63)

In Step 1, refer to the photograph for appliqué placement. For Block D, arrange the leaf spears first, then add small leaves in pairs to make a climbing vine. Machine stitch the vine stem.

Omit Step 4. In Step 5, sew a binding strip to two opposite edges of Block A. Fold the excess binding onto the wrong side, press, and glue in place. Trim the ends even with the block. Bind the two remaining edges, allowing a ¼″–⅜″ extension at each end. Fold to the wrong side and glue, tucking in the ends. Several tucks may be required. Repeat for each block.

In Step 7, trim the quilt to 24″ × 28″.

materials

1¾ yards for background and backing (Fabric 1)

4 different fabrics, each at least 10″ × 10″, for portrait blocks (Fabric 2 group)

⅓ yard for portraits binding (Fabric 3)

¼ yard for quilt binding (Fabric 4)

Assorted ⅛-yard cuts or scraps for appliqués

Assorted beads for embellishment

Thread to match or slightly contrast with appliqués

Monofilament

½ yard lightweight paper-backed fusible web

½ yard tearaway stabilizer

1¼ yards thin quilt batting or lightweight fusible batting

Quilt Diagram

butterfly garden

Butterflies and flowers are what gardens are made of. This wallhanging incorporates both of these images in true summer colors. The construction is similar to that used for the Portraits Collection quilts (pages 22–28). The background is quilted with garden foliage.

materials

1¾ yards "sky" fabric for background, backing, and binding (Fabric 1)

Assorted fabrics for portrait blocks (Fabric 2 group):

⅓ yard for Block A

¼ yard for Block B

¼ yard for Block C

⅛ yard for Block D and Block E

¼ yard for portraits binding (Fabric 3)

Assorted ⅛-yard cuts or scraps for appliqués

Assorted beads for embellishment

Thread to match or slightly contrast with appliqués

Monofilament

Thread slightly darker than background for quilting

½ yard lightweight paper-backed fusible web

½ yard tearaway stabilizer

30″ × 24½″ thin quilt batting or lightweight fusible batting, plus extra for portrait blocks

Butterfly Garden, 27½″ × 21½″, 2005, Jean Wells. Background fabric hand dyed by Mickey Lawler of Skydyes.

cutting guide

Fabric 1

BACKGROUND 30″ × 24½″

BACKING 30″ × 24½″

QUILT BINDING 2¼″ × 110″ long; omit if quilt will be professionally framed (*How to Make a Binding Strip*, page 17)

assembly

Follow steps 1–8 of the checklist on page 21.

The portrait designs are:

A Butterfly (page 66)

B Large Echinacea 1 (page 63), Large Echinacea 2 (page 64), and Large Echinacea Pair (page 64)

C Large Nine-Petal Flower (page 65)

D Multicircle Flower (page 66)

E Multicircle Flower (page 66)

In Step 4, trim the portrait blocks to the following sizes:

A $14'' \times 9''$ D $3'' \times 3''$

B $14'' \times 5''$ E $3'' \times 3''$

C $6\frac{1}{2}'' \times 11''$

In Step 7, trim the quilt to $27\frac{1}{2}'' \times 21\frac{1}{2}''$.

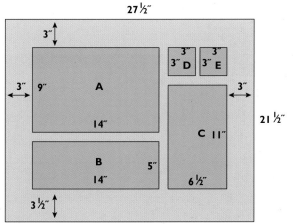

Quilt Diagram

Fabric 2 Group

Cut 5 pieces for the portrait blocks:

A $15'' \times 10''$ D $4'' \times 4''$

B $15'' \times 7''$ E $4'' \times 4''$

C $8'' \times 12''$

Fabric 3

PORTRAITS BINDING $1\frac{1}{4}'' \times 165''$ long (*How to Make a Binding Strip*, page 17)

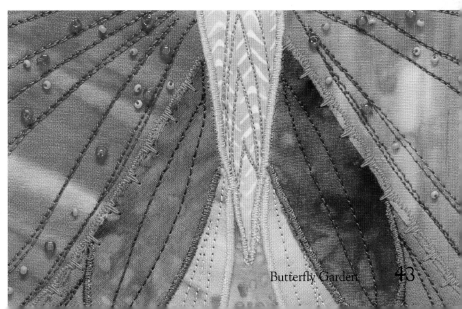

zinnias

Zinnias last the whole summer and come in a multitude of colors. They just might be my favorite flower. I made my first zinnia quilt for *Garden-Inspired Quilts*, a book I wrote with my daughter, Valori. Like many designers and artists, once I find a theme I like, I keep exploring it. For this interpretation, I used little calicoes and textured prints to create a nostalgic look. Each flower features three different fabrics, plus the gold fabric at the center. The portraits are bound with a plaid fabric from my stash that happened to have every color in my zinnias palette—a most fortunate find!

Zinnias, 33½″ × 34″, 2005, Jean Wells

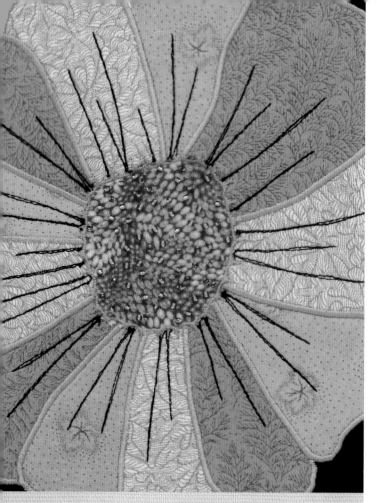

cutting guide

Fabric 1

BACKGROUND 36″ × 37″

BACKING 36″ × 37″

Fabric 2 Group

PORTRAIT BLOCKS Cut 9 pieces, each 9½″ × 9½″.

QUILT BINDING 2¼″ × 140″ long; omit if quilt will be professionally framed (*How to Make a Binding Strip*, page 17)

Fabric 3

PORTRAITS BINDING 1¼″ × 355″ long (*How to Make a Binding Strip*, page 17)

assembly

Follow steps 1–8 of the checklist on page 21.

Use the Large Zinnia pattern (page 67).

In Step 4, trim each portrait block to 8½″ × 8½″.

In Step 7, trim the quilt to 33½″ × 34″.

materials

2⅛ yards for background and backing (Fabric 1)

1¼ yards for portrait blocks and quilt binding (Fabric 2)

⅝ yards for portraits binding (Fabric 3)

Three ⅛-yard cuts or scraps for *each* flower (9 different color groups)

⅛ yard or scraps for flower centers

Assorted beads for embellishment

Thread to match or slightly contrast with appliqués

Monofilament

Thread slightly darker than background for quilting

1 yard lightweight paper-backed fusible web

1 yard tearaway stabilizer

36″ × 37″ thin quilt batting or lightweight fusible batting, plus extra for portrait blocks

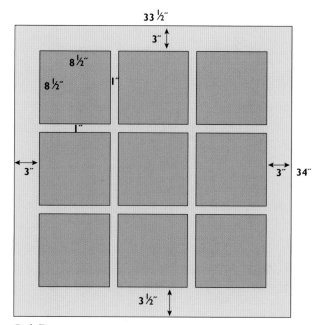

Quilt Diagram

aspen tree

Several years ago, I planted aspen trees in my garden. They provide shade in the summer and beautiful colors throughout the seasons—lime green in spring; true green in summer; yellow, orange, and rust hues in fall; and stark, skeletal beauty in winter. This quilt is my fall interpretation. My initial plan was to cut the appliquéd tree into three separate portraits, but the final design was so effective, I decided to leave it whole. I love the Asian simplicity of this piece.

materials

1¼ yards for background and backing (Fabric 1)

⅝ yard background for portrait block and quilt binding (Fabric 2)

¼ yard for portrait binding (Fabric 3)

⅜ yard for tree bark appliqué

⅛ yard of a multicolored fabric for leaves, or scraps of yellow, green, orange, and rust

Thread to match or slightly contrast with appliqués

Monofilament

Thread slightly darker than background for quilting

1 yard lightweight paper-backed fusible web

1 yard tearaway stabilizer

21″ × 39″ thin quilt batting or lightweight fusible batting, plus 13″ × 29½″ piece for portrait block

Aspen Tree, 18″ × 36″, 2005, Jean Wells

cutting guide

Fabric 1

BACKGROUND 21″ × 39″

BACKING 21″ × 39″

Fabric 2 Group

PORTRAIT BLOCK 13″ × 29½″

QUILT BINDING 2¼″ × 120″ long; omit if quilt will be professionally framed (*How to Make a Binding Strip*, page 17)

Fabric 3

PORTRAITS BINDING 1¼″ × 90″ long (*How to Make a Binding Strip*, page 17)

assembly

Follow steps 1–8 of the checklist on page 21.

Use the Aspen Tree pattern (page 68), enlarging as indicated.

In Step 4, trim the portrait block to 12″ × 28½″.

In Step 7, trim the quilt to 18″ × 36″.

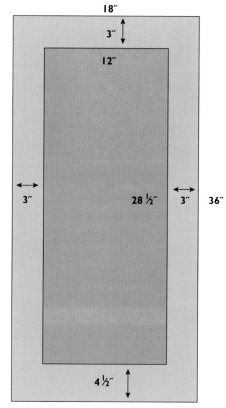

Quilt Diagram

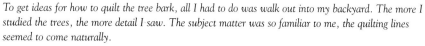

To get ideas for how to quilt the tree bark, all I had to do was walk out into my backyard. The more I studied the trees, the more detail I saw. The subject matter was so familiar to me, the quilting lines seemed to come naturally.

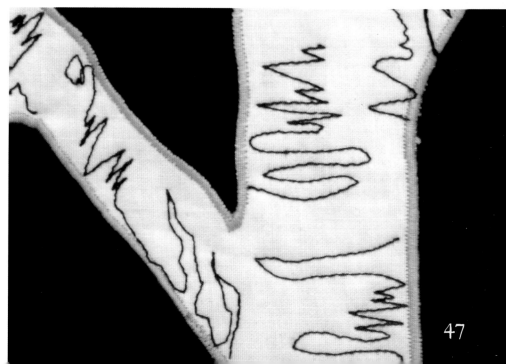

47

sunflowers of provence

Over the years, I have collected numerous pictures of the sunflower fields in Provence in France. Someday I hope to see them in person. This quilt is my interpretation of what they might look like. I focused on the flowers themselves, cropping in on the petals as if I had a camera with a zoom lens. The wavy edge on the portrait block was a work-in-progress decision. I quilted more flowers, leaves, and stems in the background to suggest endless fields. I purchased the green background fabric from a vendor at the International Quilt Festival in Houston. I like the way the light shines through the colors.

Sunflowers of Provence, 40″ × 33½″, 2005, Jean Wells

materials

2½ yards for background, backing, and binding (Fabric 1)

⅝ yard background for portrait block (Fabric 2)

¼ yard for portrait binding (Fabric 3)

⅛ yard each of 4 different yellow and yellow-gold fabrics

⅛-yard cuts or scraps of assorted brown for flower centers

¼ yard total assorted greens for stems and leaves

Assorted beads for embellishment

Thread to match or slightly contrast with appliqués

Monofilament

Thread slightly darker than background for quilting

1 yard lightweight paper-backed fusible web

1 yard tearaway stabilizer

43″ × 36½″ thin quilt batting or lightweight fusible batting, plus extra for portrait block

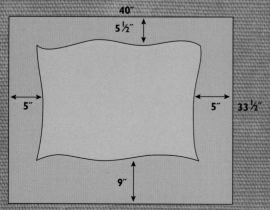

Quilt Diagram

cutting guide

Fabric 1

BACKGROUND 43″ × 36½″

BACKING 43″ × 36½″

QUILT BINDING 2¼″ × 155″ long; omit if quilt will be professionally framed (*How to Make a Binding Strip*, page 17)

Fabric 2

PORTRAIT BLOCK 30″ × 20″

Fabric 3

PORTRAIT BINDING 1¼″ × 125″ long (*How to Make a Binding Strip*, page 17)

assembly

Follow steps 1–8 of the checklist on page 21.

Use the Sunflower Petal, Sunflower Center, and Sunflower Leaf patterns (page 69).

In Step 1, cut 5 brown flower centers, 60–80 yellow and yellow-gold petals, 15 green leaves, and 5 green strips about ½″ wide for stems. Arrange a cluster of petals in a circle on an appliqué pressing sheet and add a flower center. When you are satisfied with the composition, press to fuse. Make five sunflowers total. Arrange the sunflowers, stems, and leaves on the portrait background, referring to the project photograph for placement ideas. Fuse in place.

In steps 2 and 3, use stitching and beads to make each sunflower center different.

In Step 4, use a rotary cutter to freehand cut a wavy line along each edge of the portrait block. Crop in on some of the sunflowers for a zoom-lens view.

In Step 5, bind each edge separately, without mitering the corners. Fold the excess binding onto the reverse side and secure with a glue stick.

In Step 7, trim the quilt to 40″ × 33½″.

shadow boxes

When I spotted beautifully made shadow boxes at Pottery Barn, I immediately saw the possibilities for framing individual portrait blocks. Each box came with four ball-head straight pins, which I used to mount a label and my quilted work. The 1″ depth allowed me to display dimensional items, too, like the poppy seed pods I saved from last summer's garden. These two projects sew up quickly and make unique gifts.

materials

11″ × 9″ shadow box

7″ × 9″ rectangle for portrait (Fabric 2)

¼ yard for portrait binding (Fabric 3)

⅛ yard or scraps for appliqués

Assorted rocailles and/or bugle beads for embellishment

Thread to match or slightly contrast with appliqués

⅛ yard lightweight paper-backed fusible web

¼ yard tearaway stabilizer

¼ yard thin quilt batting or lightweight fusible batting

Maple Leaves

11″ × 9″ × 1″ deep, 2005, Jean Wells

I found a vibrant hand-dyed fabric for these leaf appliqués—it was fun deciding which part of the fabric to use! Fabric 2 is a watery purple color with subtle stripes. Fabric 3 is a darker, richer purple; prepare 36″ of portrait binding from this fabric.

Follow steps 1–5 of the checklist on page 21.

In Step 1, trace the Maple Leaf pattern (page 68) or photocopy a real leaf and make a tracing. The leaf size and quantity don't really matter, because the appliqués are cropped at the edges for a zoom-lens effect.

In Step 2, sew two rows of straight stitching almost on top of each other for the leaf stems.

In Step 3, sew rocailles along sewn vein lines.

In Step 4, trim the portrait block to 6″ × 8″.

Himalayan Poppy

9″ × 11″ × 1″ deep, 2005, Jean Wells

The poppy appliqué has became a favorite of mine. Inspired by a photo in a seed catalog, I chose light aqua fabric for the petals, yellow for the flower center, and green for the stem. Fabric 2 features deep teal tones. For a sophisticated finish, I used solid black for Fabric 3; prepare 30″ of portrait binding from this fabric.

Follow steps 1–5 of the checklist on page 21.

In Step 1, use the Poppy pattern (page 59).

In Step 3, sew six yellow bugle beads to the flower center.

In Step 4, trim the portrait block to 5″ × 6″.

patterns

Determine which patterns you want to use in the portrait blocks. The patterns in this book may be reduced or enlarged if you wish to customize the quilt.

Remember, the patterns will reverse themselves when fused in place. See Sketchbook on pages 6–7 for more information on creating original designs. If you wish to reverse a design, trace it on tracing paper with a fine-point Sharpie pen, then turn it over. You will be able to see the black line through the tracing paper. Place the paper-backed adhesive over the drawing and trace the shape.

Leaf

Bud

Starflower

Trace and cut out petals as a single unit.

Gloxinia

Droopy Sunflower 1

Trio

Wide Leaf

Chrysanthemum

Cut 10

Leaf Duo

Slender Leaf

54   Portraits From Nature

Leaf Trio

Slender Leaf Trio

Leafy Garden

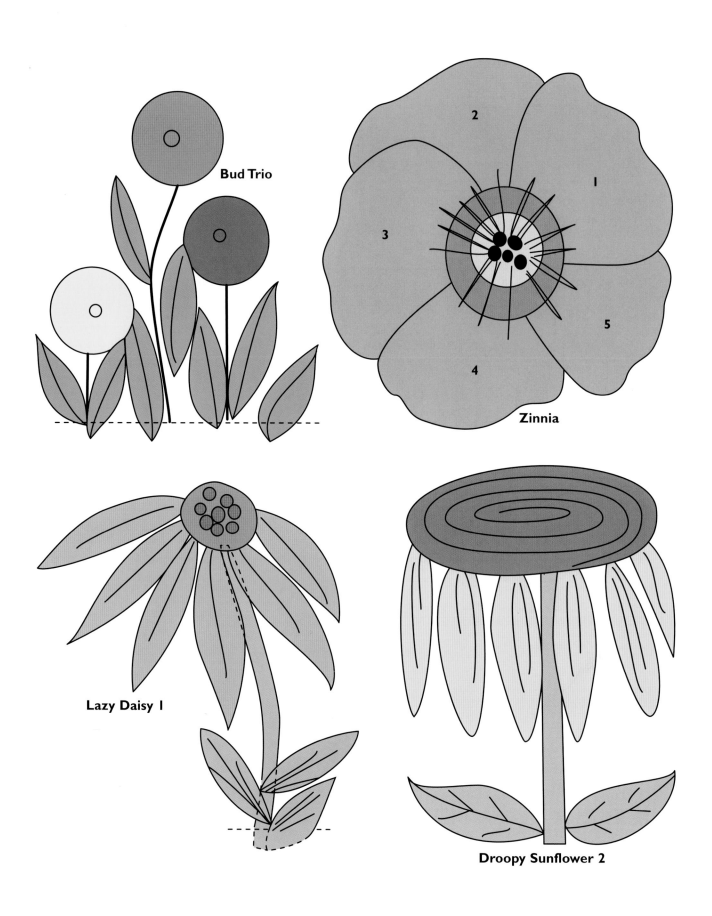

Bud Trio

Zinnia

Lazy Daisy 1

Droopy Sunflower 2

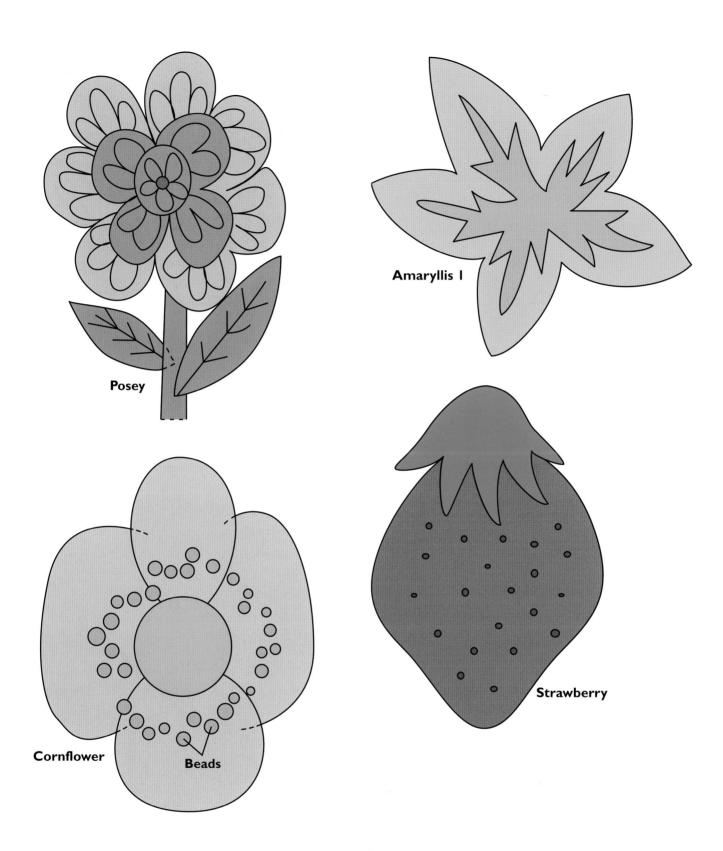

Posey

Amaryllis I

Cornflower

Beads

Strawberry

Amaryllis 2

Wildflowers

Wild Berries

Woodland Flowers

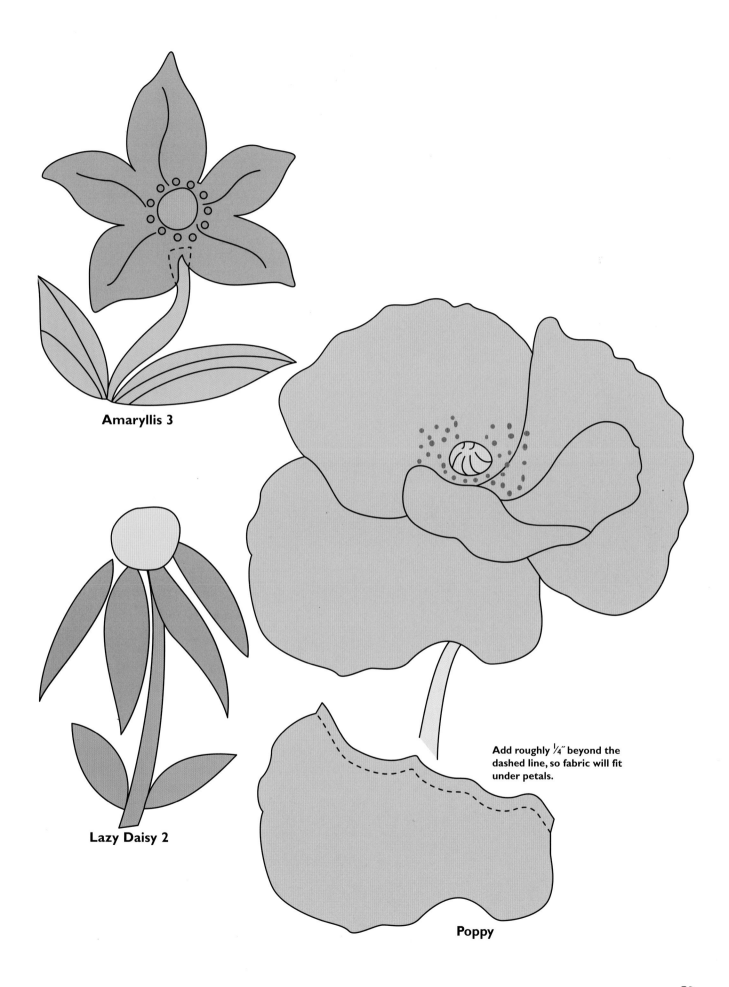

Amaryllis 3

Lazy Daisy 2

Add roughly ¼″ beyond the
dashed line, so fabric will fit
under petals.

Poppy

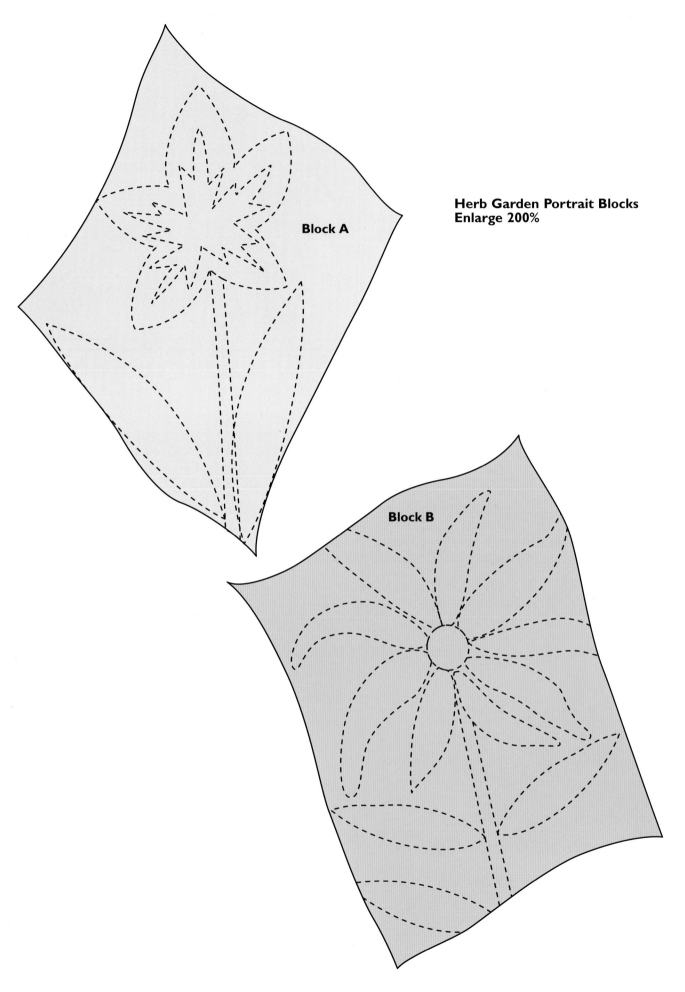

**Herb Garden Portrait Blocks
Enlarge 200%**

Block A

Block B

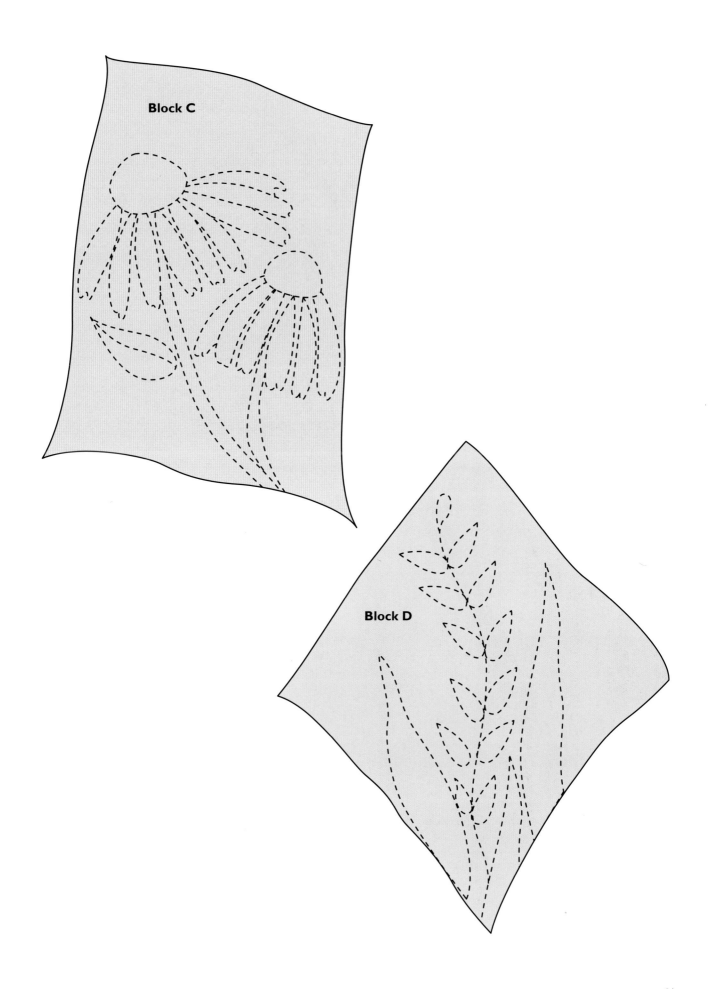

Block C

Block D

Five-Petal Flower

Cut second leaf in reverse

Portraits From Nature

Small Leaves

Leaf Spears

Large Echinacea 1

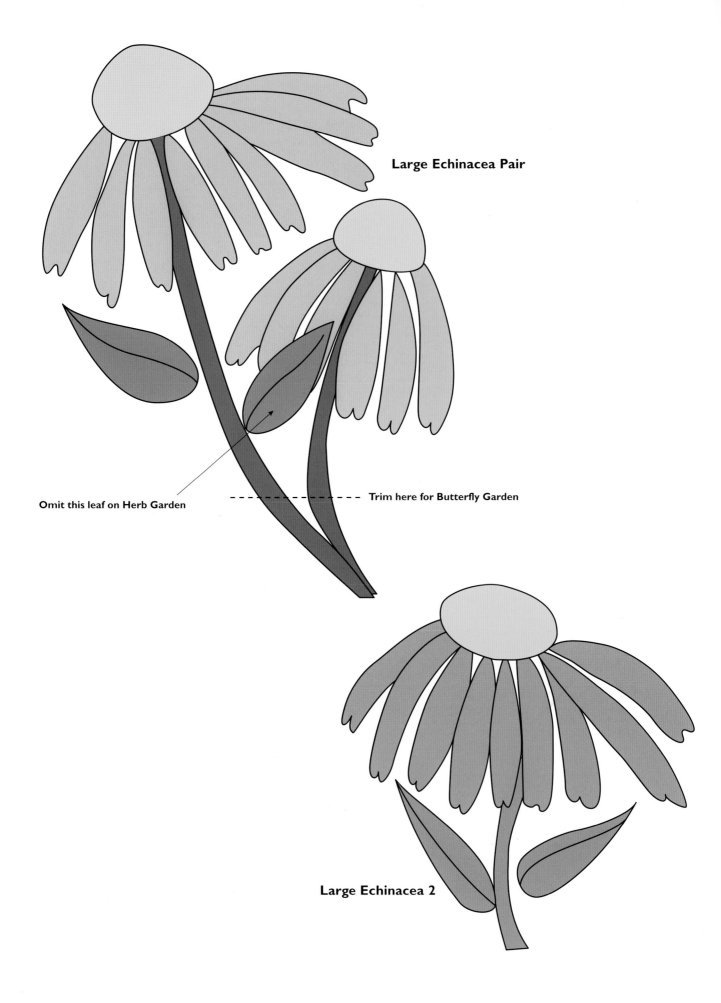

Large Echinacea Pair

Omit this leaf on Herb Garden

- - - - - - - - - - - Trim here for **Butterfly Garden**

Large Echinacea 2

**Large Nine-Petal Flower
Enlarge 120%**

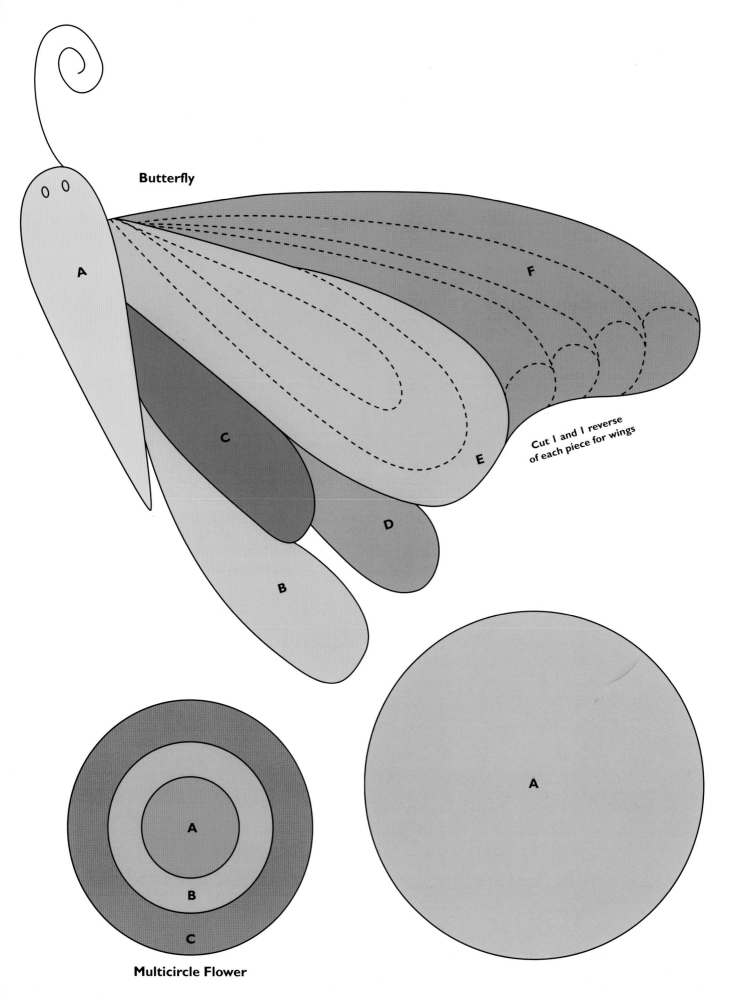

Butterfly

A

C

B

D

E

F

Cut I and I reverse
of each piece for wings

Multicircle Flower

A

B

C

A

Portraits From Nature

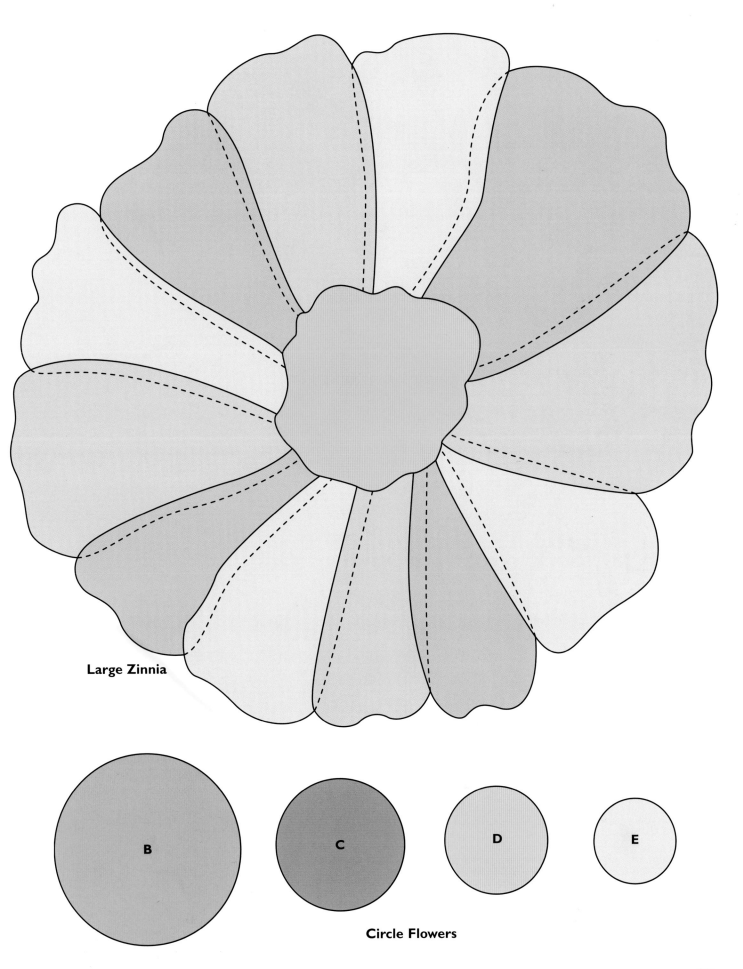

Large Zinnia

Circle Flowers

Aspen Tree
Enlarge 275%

Maple Leaf

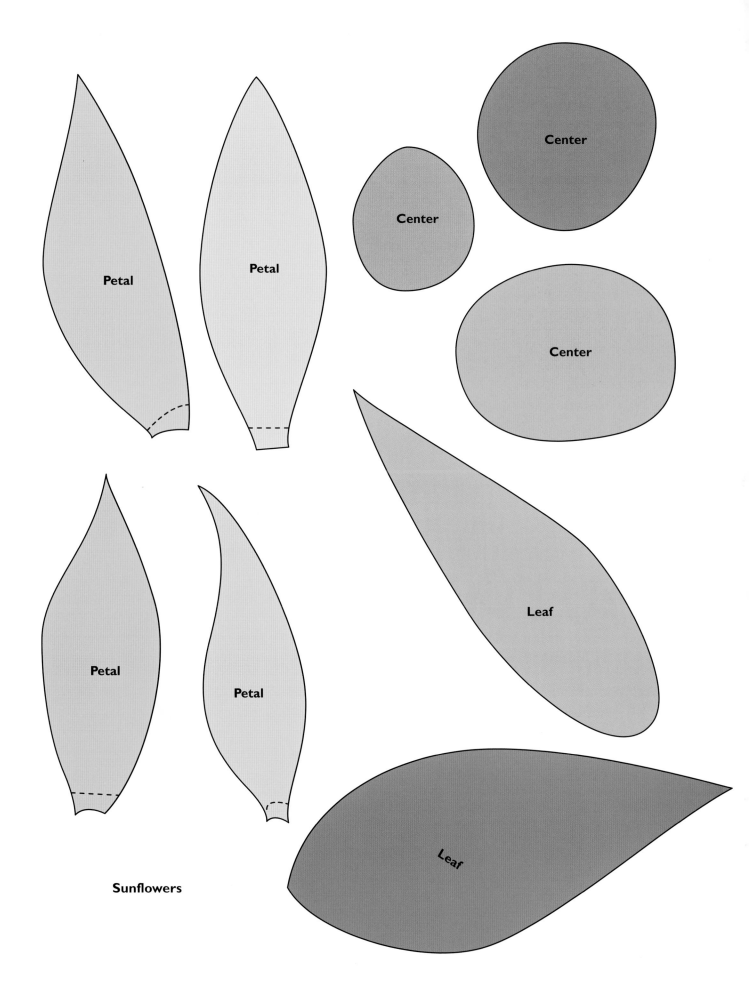

Sunflowers

index

sources

The Stitchin' Post
PO Box 280
311 West Cascade Street
Sisters, OR 97759
541-549-6061
www.stitchinpost.com
stitchin@stitchinpost.com

The Wild Hare
PO Box 280
321 West Cascade Street
Sisters, OR 97759
541-549-6061

The Cotton Patch
1025 Brown Avenue, Dept CTB
Lafayette, CA 94549
www.quiltusa.com
cottonpatch@quiltusa.com

Cotton Ginny's
575 W. Amber Way
Hanford, CA 93230
www.cottonginnys.com

Pottery Barn
www.potterybarn.com

Skydyes
PO Box 370116
West Hartford, CT 06137-0116
fabrics@skydyes.com
www.skydyes.com
Mickey Lawler

about the author

Gardens and quilting have been a constant inspiration to Jean Wells for decades. This talented quilter has written 27 books on quilting subjects, including *Patchwork Quilts Made Easy* and the new Oh Sew Easy soft furnishing series, developed in collaboration with her daughter Valori. All of Jean's books reflect her friendly, approachable teaching style and her love of color and design. As co-owner with Valori of The Stitchin' Post in Sisters, Oregon, Jean is in close contact with quilters of all levels, a connection she relishes for fresh ideas and inspiration. Jean's quilts have been featured on television shows and in magazines, and she has traveled the world teaching others the joy of quilting. At home, she enjoys being grandma to Braden and Olivia Rose; helping with the Sisters Outdoor Quilt Show, held annually the second Saturday in July; and simply puttering in her garden, coming up with more quilts to plant.

Great Titles
from C&T PUBLISHING

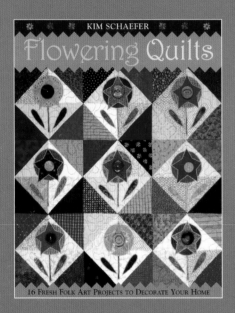

KIM SCHAEFER

Flowering Quilts

16 FRESH FOLK ART PROJECTS TO DECORATE YOUR HOME

JOEN WOLFROM

A Garden Party of Quilts

7 PIECED PROJECTS FOR FLOWER LOVERS

FUSING FUN!
Fast Fearless Art Quilts

LAURA WASILOWSKI

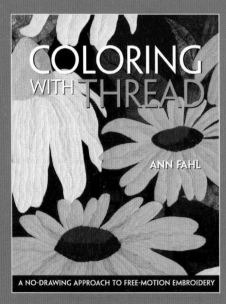

COLORING WITH THREAD

ANN FAHL

A NO-DRAWING APPROACH TO FREE-MOTION EMBROIDERY

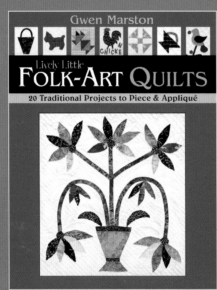

Gwen Marston

Lively Little
FOLK-ART QUILTS

20 Traditional Projects to Piece & Appliqué

All-in-One
Beading Buddy

All-in-One
Beading Buddy

The **ultimate** beading reference tool!

Easy to use

Bead Guide

Stitch Index

• 78 Beading Stitches
• Step-by-Step Instructions
• Helpful Tips and How-To's
• Bonus-Value Finder

IDEAL FOR:
Beading
Quilting
Scrapbooking
Embroidery
Wearables
Crafts
Home Décor

Mary Stori